The Curse of the Square Crow

Poems by Dick Dixon
Drawings by Reine Mazoyer

Mereo Books

2nd Floor, 6-8 Dyer Street, Cirencester, Gloucestershire, GL7 2PF
An imprint of Memoirs Books. www.mereobooks.com
and www.memoirsbooks.co.uk

The Curse of the Square Crow: 978-1-86151-954-2

First published in Great Britain in 2019

© Poems - Dick Dixon
© Illustrations - Reine Mazoyer

The address for Memoirs Books can be
found at www.mereobooks.com

Mereo Books Ltd. Reg. No. 12157152

Typeset in 13/18pt Malgun Gothic
by Wiltshire Associates. Printed and bound in Great Britain

CONTENTS

Explication en francais

PREFACE

Readers of 'Rhymes for no Reason' or 'The Rimes of the Newfangled Mariner', previous books of verse by Dick Dixon and illustrated by Reine Mazoyer, may see no reason to continue their journey in this present volume, though I do believe that this could be a huge mistake. I mean to say – where else could you read about a cat that plays the piano, or how to cheer up a depressed octopus; how to approach a crocodile made of handbag leather, and how to enjoy your year more by making the summer longer and the winter shorter – and even what strategy to adopt if captured by Martians? This is just a tiny sample of the problems encountered and dealt with, at least to some small extent, in this latest volume.

It is true that not many of the unusual situations we find here are hi-tech, but definitely tech of a lower order, and are also echoes perhaps of an earlier time. Even so, I am sure that that does not mean that they are any less interesting.

The book may remind us of times in the near past when people had more direct human contact, social media had not been invented, and instead of texting or emailing a friend or relative across the room, one might even consider, and take pleasure in, rising from one's chair in order to take a trek of as much as ten yards (now metres, if you please!) in order to indulge in a face-to-face experience. People exist today for whom this is unthinkable; what will become of us?

That was one reason for writing the books – to make an attempt at portraying ourselves in a more homely way, and rather more in keeping with how we used to be until recently, and to jog our memories about the good 'friendly neighbourhood' qualities our society assumed perhaps rather casually. There are certainly many reasons to wish to preserve and cherish the good things that have evolved through many centuries of our society, while being aware of the 'not so good'. These good things of course include tolerance, sympathy, kindness, unselfishness and generally thinking of others first – and of course good humour. How easily it seems that these things can be lost. Quite often, when I mention this kind of thing to people, mostly younger ones I come across in my daily life as a teacher, they give me a look that seems to show that they are wondering if I am 'on something', or perhaps have just landed from another planet. Sometimes they do agree with me, which is encouraging.

Anyway, I would not be at all surprised if gently humorous poetry, which is what many of the verses here are intended to be, is a positive thing – even though a darker element may creep in to some of them on occasion. Many writers of the past have thought so, in any case.

A few giants of the past, veritable pioneers of humorous verse that come to mind, are Lewis Carroll, Edward Lear, Mervyn Peake, and more recently Roald Dahl and Spike Milligan. I'm sure that a substantial number of readers of English today will remember their work with fondness. Such reading and writing of humorous verse I hope may encourage us to think about how we react towards each other in our daily lives, and perhaps help us to empathise better. All right – it's a vain hope, but hey, we have nothing to lose by trying it, wouldn't you say?

Even if animals are involved in these poems, by the way, they are treated as though they are 'alternative humans'. Nobody pretends (at least I hope not!) that they understand what an octopus, crocodile or elephant is thinking about, or even whether they are thinking at all, if 'thinking' is the right word – but because we are human, we can imagine something of how they might 'think' if they were human too, and by magically endowing animals with those qualities, we learn more about our own human qualities, I expect.

We have tried to order the poems a little, so that the more light-hearted ones are concentrated towards the earlier parts of the book, while the later part contains a denser sprinkling of slightly more serious ones. Reine Mazoyer has done her usual brilliant job of illustrating the poems in glorious colour, and I have to say that this has been a difficult task sometimes, as the subject matter is sometimes very hard to deal with in pictures. Reine comes through with 'flying colours' every time.

Well, the time for philosophy is over. As a famous man once said, 'Let us now bend ourselves to our task', or something very similar – which in this case is to read on!

May we wish you good luck – we hope you enjoy the book, and let us hope that you are free of the curse of the Square Crow, poor thing.

Dick Dixon

August 2020

The Curse of the Square Crow

THE SQUARE CROW

The square crow is unfortunate,
In several ways – at least!
Of course, he's really cubical,
This ill-constructed beast,
But never mind – what's in a name?
A crow's a crow – it's all the same.

The square crow's in a grimmish mood,
At every time of day,
For being square is quite a trial,
And wipes his smile away;
It's rather painful when he walks,
And square tongues are no help to talk.

And having square legs hardly helps,
Except perhaps at cricket,
But square crows do not care for it,
Just standing near the wicket –
As crippling as it is to run,
Though normal crows no doubt have fun.

'And can the square crow fly?' you ask;
The answer's not quite clear.
It all depends what's meant by flight,
But luckily he has no fear,
Though square wings make it rather hard
To fly much more than just a yard.

Which is a pity, don't you think?
And would be compensation,
For inability to run,
Or walk to Hampstead Station –
If he's a London crow of course;
A country crow could ride a horse!

But for the city crow you see,
There's another way to go:
Taxis, vans and cars provide
Roofs for perching, long and low;
The square crow need not spend a sou,
Although of course there'll be no loo!

But now the worst part must be told:
The square crow lives in horror
That one day he, or really she –
Must square up to the mirror,
And search the square crow soul for courage;
At least – as much as she can manage.

It's destiny that shapes crows' ends,
And square crows are likewise;
But somehow strength must now be found,
An inward tide of gall must rise –
No use to cry out, plead or beg:
She's got to lay her first square egg!

THE PHOTOGRAPH

A panel slides, and there it is,
And was for decades there concealed,
Attached by brittle sticky tape
By one whose hand lies white and dead,
To the cold and crumbling wall revealed;
But time has passed on, passed ahead
Unsung, and made its slow escape.

A photograph in black and white:
People sitting on a beach,
Sprawling, smiling on the sands.
They cannot know who suffers pain,
Safely gone, and out of reach;
Immortalised in silver grain,
And touching with glad eyes and hands.

They're relatives I never met,
And if news came, the moon was blue;
They never knew, and never spoke
About this child; nor did I exist
That day, to them: was I in Peru?
I light a match, in mental mist,
And find catharsis in the smoke.

THE LOVE OF BEANS

The love life of the jumping bean,
From ancient Mexico,
Is dangerous beyond belief;
At least, it does seem so.

For beans on heat must first locate,
From deep within their shells,
A sympathetic urging mate,
With whom to 'kiss and tell'.

And this is not, I'll tell you now,
An easy thing to do;
It's dark in there – you can't see out;
You're hot and bothered too!

It's lucky that these beans have ears,
To listen for a friend;
The sound they're listening for is 'boing' –
Then – know which way to wend.

The problem is: both beans go 'boing',
And bounce they know not where,
So hard it is to make contact
They might meet in the air!

The other thing, it must be said,
Is lack of arms to hold
Each other in the throes of love,
So their bodies need to mould.

Then are they suited anyway?
As neither one has seen
Inside the other's shell just yet,
To check it's no 'has bean'!

It's not surprising, you'll agree,
That jumping beans are rare;
It's just too hard to reproduce –
I wonder if they care.

But never mind – beans thrive elsewhere;
And in Britain we can boast,
Not perhaps of jumping beans,
But we've got beans on toast!

THE BLUES

There was a time when
It was thought quite fit,
That I should sit
Before a large black box,
Engaging, but enraging
At the monochrome display –
Joanna, wooden woman of the room,
Who lives there as I write today,
And oh so quietly mocks.

Endless scales that no
Fish had ever seen,
In a sea or stream,
Nor ever at the ends of piers –
Empty houses on both sides,
More police cars than were needed
I would say, but then again I'm biased;
'I'll never need this', I pleaded,
To deaf determined ears.

The spots and rods that
Graced the written page,
Led the way to rage,
Or loss, at least of hope,
That making sense might not be hard,
That music might arrive by writ –
But were not Gershwin, Brahms and Chaminade
Abased by clumsy fingers, scarcely fit
To do much more than grope?

One day, as I crept down
The stairs in pensive mood,
Sounds came from the wood
That were delight in fact;
A beautiful cadenza
Was being played for me
It seemed, and I marvelled that it could
Be done, and even more you see,
That the guilty party was the cat.

IN THE SOUP

'Too many cooks spoil the broth.'
So could we make do with just one?
No doubt we'll need pepper,
Though nutmeg is better,
For the finest broth under the sun.

The question is: which one to choose?
As they stand in a row by the pot.
The best are the ones in white hats,
So stiffened by starch, in their spats –
But those in black boots – maybe not!

It is quite an honour of course,
To be chosen for 'Dish of the Year',
But you know that your mission
Is just vaulting ambition –
You'll be glad that your fame is so near.

The event will go down in the books,
And regaled in the decades to come;
This astonishing dish –
Well, what more could one wish?
In respect, we'll be rendered quite dumb.

In conclusion, we offer our thanks,
To our cook, whose stature will grow,
As he walks the few feet
In green garnish discreet,
Then dives in the pot – what a pro!

DISCOVERY!

Though I love her with a passion uncontrolled,
And that this might ever change I cannot see,
It's unlikely that I'll ever understand her,
When she dries her just-washed undies in a tree.

But if I'm ever tempted to chastise her,
I am brought up very short in shuddering jolts,
As to her we owe a handsome cache of rubies,
And also several tons of Solomon's gold.

For once, on the hottest day of summer,
I saw her drying wish fall foul in spades,
When, having hung her knickers in a plum tree,
She later spewed an angry blue tirade.

It was rather sad to witness her distresses;
Such days of heat are seldom sent entire,
But for all the bitter tears that soaked her tresses,
At least we know how man discovered fire!

DRESSING DOWN

When Monday comes around to call,
Dragging grey clouds in her wake,
We rise from dream-time pillows all,
With limbs of lead and brains of cake;
Then a pain, mid solar plexus –
Work again! It surely wrecks us.

Got up once more in fancy gear:
Stiff collars, links, and studs and ties;
For ladies, just-so skirts and hair
In style to bounce round shadowed eyes;
With polished shoes and morning face,
We step outside to join the race.

That's not of course the human race;
It takes the week to reach that state.
Just battling through the Monday maze
Will shatter nerves and make us late –
On arrival, each a zombie,
Yet aware that there'll be Friday.

Friday, oh Friday – do say it again,
Friday, how hallowed is truly thy name;
Down a long tunnel of darkness and drain,
We struggle in chains to find your bright flame.
Life, it is certain, could not be much gorier –
Then Friday is here: In Excelsis, Gloria!

Off with your tie-pins and sensible skirts;
Out with your cuff-links: you know it makes sense.
Kick off those high heels and rip off white shirts;
Fear no reprisals – this could be immense!
On the stroke of four-thirty, lower the lights,
As we dance round the cauldron in undies and tights.

Give us Scotch whisky and coke by the ton;
Blast the fifth floor with the heaviest rock –
Mystical happenings – all will be one –
Then all fall exhausted – one eye on the clock;
But now bells are ringing – it's seven again,
And we're waking on Monday to thunder and rain.

FIVE A DAY

Oh – have you had your 'five a day'?
One's not enough, I've heard them say,
Nor two, nor three nor even four
They chant – then bear your corpse away.

You say you must survive the day?
Not run the risk you'll pass away?
If so, make sure your fruit is near,
Enough to last you through the year.

As well you need fresh veg to eat –
Include them in your daily treat;
I hope the total's more than four,
To curb your maker's wish to meet.

It's wise though not to go too far
Beyond the 'rule of five' – the bar;
Common sense must be applied,
Or danger lurks in your inside.

An instance here of this good creed,
To use in case of doubt or greed:
You may consume ten pumpkin seeds –
Ten pumpkins though, you'll never need!

CROCODILLY CIRCUS

I met a crocodile last week,
Whose skin was of red leather –
Made from handbags and old straps,
Arranged and stitched together.

He spoke in perfect croc lingo
I was able to translate,
Though clearly he'd spent time abroad,
Or was my vocab out of date?

In any case we managed to
Communicate our thoughts,
And spoke with gusto all about
So many things of different sorts.

At length he raised the subject of
His curious construction;
Was he a 'crocodile in the room'?
That at least was my deduction!

Bizarre indeed it was to see
A croc of handbag leather,
And I confessed my great surprise –
Though at least he had no feathers.

As he went on, he claimed, no less,
It was not superficial –
Not just his skin, but all the rest;
It seemed somehow official.

As though the universe might seem
Maladjusted and deficient,
Without his contribution
To some unknown coefficient.

I wondered then how we could test
His inner parts concealed,
And proposed – with his permission,
I might delve; would that appeal?

He shook and snorted with a shriek
That could only mean one thing –
Oh reader, if you'd been there,
It would have made you sing!

Thus it was that as the sun
Slipped slowly down the sky,
I asked him – with no trace of fear,
To relax, and open wide.

Whereupon I gently slipped
My fingers, wrist and forearm,
Past his leather teeth and tongue,
In earnest hope that he'd be charmed.

Down the red-ribbed throat my arm
Slid down with ease – quite straight, not bent;
He gave me just a tiny wink,
To confirm his clear enjoyment.

It was indeed a great success,
As even at the furthest throw,
Every tiny body part was
The finest leather you could know.

And that's not all; I must report
More findings from there too:
As I withdrew my questing arm
Four odd things hove into view.

From nestling in the leather pouch,
Which had been their former home,
I brought to light a tiny mirror,
Mascara, lipstick and a comb.

HOW LONG?

Out of time, another dream:
I wait, ensconced in deep-green grass,
The weak sun spinning woeful rays
Through bars of tearful grey.
Huge and hungry white birds scream
At the breeze, in descent as they pass;
But the whirl of the wind very soon,
In new regulation of time,
Follows beams of the haunted moon
All down the beaches of brass,
All down the hills, burnt in their prime,
To the dales, pale acres in lime.
Oh, for the fretwork of stars
In the honeyed wilderness –
And oh, to be seized in the hours
When the throb of the ancient land
Gives forth its abundance of flowers!

But when the seagulls are full,
Replete from the swell of the sea,
And the fish are left gasping but free –
That, that is when we shall see
Yet again the number 3B,
To the lovely Linden by Lea.
Oh, here it is now, waiting for me,
Over there, by the old apple tree.

*The reader may well have had similar thoughts while
awaiting the arrival of the 3B. I know I have!*

HEAVEN ON EARTH

I lay beneath the spreading sky
On summer grass in June –
The dome a thousand miles of blue,
Though no bird sang a tune;
It seemed that all the clocks were stopped,
Yet the years had stripped away,
And suddenly I found myself
A child once more, that day.

The time and sun suspended in
The sky of yesteryear,
Gave no hint that you had come
To be again so near –
But of course in fact 'twas I
Who'd wished to fill that void of blue:
To be again as once we were,
When I was close to you.

Dark years and long ago in school,
We were scarcely seven,
And nowadays I often think
Of you, quite safe in heaven –
Taken from us as you were,
As tulips bloomed in spring;
Please Gillian, before we part,
Please take with you this ring.

At primary school in the mid-fifties, a delightful little girl in my class was taken suddenly one day to hospital with appendicitis. Very sadly, she died soon afterwards. I often think about this tragedy, even these days.

LAMENT OF THE WALRUS

'I'm getting up', the walrus said,
'To many tricks these days;
Long weeks have passed since I could meet
Your scrutiny and gaze,
And now I find I cannot be
The bearer of good news –
My thoughts of old supplanted now,
By newer dreams of zoos.'

'Now cabbages I cannot stand,
And I've yet to meet a king –
And sealing wax is only good
For pressing with a ring.
While shoes and ships are fine per se,
I cannot say I'm struck,
As all I seem to want these days,
Is a van, or maybe truck.'

'To take me back where I belong –
The heart of London Zoo;
It's where I feel I am at home,
Along with kangaroos,
And seals and lions, and parakeets
From distant Ecuador,
And oh, to dine on oysters then,
On each weekday at four.'

'So keep your ships and sealing-wax,
Your cabbages and shoes,
Just send my tusks and whiskers home,
There's little time to lose –
But just one thing that's on my mind
Is how I can contrive,
To get the van to London Zoo –
This walrus cannot drive!'

I feel I must offer some sort of apology to Lewis Carroll for taking his creations in vain in such a cavalier manner. Fortunately the carpenter was able to make good his escape!

THE DILEMMA

When Cousin Prue had time to spare,
She felt the urge to travel:
To feel cool wind on hair and face,
Dark stresses to unravel.

Her burden was that since childhood,
She'd had a tinted skin;
And strange to say, pale green it was,
Like gin and lime, without the gin.

So where to go? She had no clue,
No inspiration came,
But on a bus to town she saw
An advert written in a frame.

"Come to happy 'Sunnyside'",
It said in letters bold;
"You'll need to take your clothes off,
But in June it won't be cold".

Prue thought this over night and day;
Could it be her scene?
Perhaps the sun would tan her skin,
To banish by degrees the hated green.

She made a firm decision then,
To do it, and to hell
With all the prudish types she knew;
Upon her mind was cast a spell.

After all, Prue knew she had
A body that most girls
Would have surrendered eye-teeth for,
Or all their blonde and baby curls.

She knew this from another time,
When waking in the bath;
The water'd long before run out,
Yet male admirers beat a path!

So off Prue went, the tenth of June,
By car to 'Sunnyside',
As the sun blazed forth on overtime,
And blessed, but boiled her on her ride.

In her room at journey's end,
Time for a final check:
Prue slipped off her underwear –
Was her body just a wreck?

Not at all, though still pale green,
She saw her bust was full;
With female curves to make her proud,
Prue had never felt less dull!

Everything was all arranged,
All ready for the mingling,
With tons of other naked flesh;
She soon was almost tingling.

With confidence, Prue slid downstairs
As quietly as she could,
Into the garden where the guests
Chatted naked where they stood.

Each guest sipped from a crystal glass,
But the conversation paused,
When first my cousin showed herself –
And raised a round of loud applause!

Then in a thunderbolt, Prue gasped
At the sunny evening scene;
Not that the guests wore birthday suits,
But more that all were shades of green!

THE PENDULUM

There's no point in asking –
I haven't a clue,
I'm in complete darkness,
Even more so than you.

It's quite a long story,
You won't want to hear,
Unless I provide you
With pretzels and beer.

But would you believe it,
If I spilled the beans?
In fact though – I told you,
I don't have the means.

And as you will notice,
I am in no shape,
To provide any drinks,
Until I escape.

I just hope the weather
Will be warm without rain,
Or the coming of night
Will be quite a pain.

You realise I woke up
This morning like this,
But now I remember –
Connubial bliss.

At least it was mentioned –
It does ring a bell,
But my lady has vanished –
The best man as well!

The night they invented
Champagne was not good;
It's led to my downfall,
And less than good mood.

But please have some mercy –
Just think how you'd feel,
If you had my problem –
Not part of the deal!

So many feet up from
The ground with no hope,
Inverted and dangling
At the end of a rope!

A NEW CALENDAR

It's best three winter months be short;
Let's say twenty days, no more,
As Jack Frost nips and all is dark,
And toes and noses turn red raw.
Now global warming's here to stay,
We'll welcome early spring – hooray!

Bring on March and April now;
Give them twenty-five days each.
Let wind and rain disturb the trees,
But air endow with power of speech –
To whisper promise of new life,
As wakes the frozen earth from strife.

Now come lovely May and June;
Let eight and thirty days each mark.
While gardens gush forth greenery,
Behold the tulip and the lark,
And tiny buds now flowered in full –
As lambs fill frenzied fields with wool.

The next three months have forty days,
While summer's heat gains fearsome grip:
The devil drives our pressing need,
Though bodies burn and skin is stripped.
The ultra-violet makes us brown,
But folds each face in deep-fried frown.

The last two months see autumn rain:
Reduce their count to thirty days.
Now nights draw in their cramp and cold,
And days are full of damp and haze;
We tramp through fields of murk and mud,
Which scarcely shifts our sullen blood.

Now all is done in numbered days,
With one in hand if not leap year,
But winter's short and summer long –
Is this not then the course to steer?
Or would you fight with might and main,
To suffer more – to be in pain?

Let not blind habit forge our ways;
The old must usher in the new.
Just hold your breath and take a leap –
All will soon be tickety-boo.
Note well that omelettes cannot be,
Unless some eggs are broken – see?

THE BULLDOG BREED

When a bulldog chews a wasp,
It has no thought of diet,
Yet some small fragment of its brain
Exhorts it to 'please try it'.

For in that buzzing insect,
There lies a cache of gold –
A certain special something,
That dogs need, so it's told.

But a bulldog's brain is tiny,
And the dog is unaware,
That a thousand years of wisdom
Repose so deep in there.

What a price your dog must pay,
The pain of sores and stings,
But even so, it must be done,
To reach for higher things.

The wasp will die with honour,
Though never know quite why,
But in another thousand years,
I dare say dogs might fly!

SLEEPLESS NIGHTS

Oh, but the burdens of this fallen world
Echo and rock around my reeling head –
While the canopy of stars pulsates with light
Too dim to show the way to fitful bed;
There'll be another night of slumber steeped
In cold and heavy clay that aches and weeps
Through haunted dreams and broken shallow sleep.

As night wears on, I think of other worlds,
Where justice, truth and mercy may prevail –
Though on this earth, those heads are hidden well,
And good intent is lost along the trail.
I'll toss and turn and watch the changing skies
Of mauve and blue that match my troubled soul,
Until bright sun once more exacts its toll.

'Enough!' I cry – solutions there must be,
Though not perhaps for all by life oppressed,
But surely so for those in lack of sleep –
Let the compass point us all to well-earned rest.
Might musing of the mind make mental sheep,
To save the day – or better still, the night,
And rescue us from this nocturnal plight?

Maybe sheep that can be counted give some hope,
Though not know of course they'd serve a noble cause;
Perhaps tonight's the night to summon strength –
To conjure up a vision on the moors,
Of milling ovine beasts at turf and brook;
Bucolic is the scene – I heave a sigh;
Let counting now begin in my mind's eye.

It's thankless work, I'll readily confess,
As sheep of mind I've found do not comply
With irksome limits set out for their scene:
The truth is that they're not inclined to try,
And meander, a white and scattered stream,
And though I might the sheepish mind enhance,
These stubborn creatures just seek greener grass!

Counting's cold confusion and so vexed,
And not as soporific as desired –
Why would the arms of Morpheus extend
To one whose count is underhand, and mired
In doubt – augmented by the hour?
Another path is needed – that is clear,
To total sheep and lambs without a fear.

I now admit: a smile has crossed my face;
The answer glares back at me from the ground:
It is to score a mark upon each fleece,
And thus record a total that is sound.
May the gods of slumber grace with sleep my head,
To see their servant's work writ large in red –
From the pot of paint that lies beside the bed.

THE PREDICAMENT

I have thought so long and hard
Of several different things
That traverse my tiny fevered brain.
Dwindling is my wish to sing,
In the struggle with my wings;
My composure is unlikely to remain.

The problem that besets me
Is one you wouldn't mind,
I dare say, it now occurs to me;
Whether crooked, cruel or kind,
You'd regard my kind of bind,
As one you'd solve in seconds after tea.

It would soon occur to you
To elevate your feet,
And walk your sticky way towards the edge,
Then tip your tub of meat
Upon the tablecloth so neat,
Then as usual, simply go and trim the hedge.

Or something of the kind,
In your everyday routine –
I do wish my legs were only two;
An upright human being,
Just has no eyes for seeing
The pain we insects often must go through.

Look – my legs total six,
And rely on my own power,
So I'm not sure I'll ever see my feet.
I can lift one in an hour,
Then the problem seems to tower;
It's a hopeless case I want to solve 'tout de suite'.

Would it be so bad,
If my plight could never see
The light, or even darkness of the day?
Could a fly become a bee,
Or the ointment beer or Brie,
In countless other better things to say
Than this horrid idiom,
That's caused me pain? It's true!
Though in my mind the answer surely lurks;
As from my point of view,
We should chop it, sans ado:
Just restrict ourselves to 'spanner in the works'.

THE SHAKING CURSE

"It seems to me," she croaked, wide-eyed,
"I need to take advice."
Her suit was green as grass in May,
With pockets bursting full of dice.
"Can you not see I shake today,
Though never have I seen your mice?"

But no mice had I at the time
Nor anything to fear,
Except the huge red hat I wore,
Though no other matching gear.
Her tremor though was plain to see;
I offered her a beetroot beer.

"Thank you, no", she breathed in pain,
"It makes my shaking worse";
I suggested then that in that case,
We work at once to ban her curse.
"Yes indeed" came forth with speed,
"I wish no more to need a nurse!"

I ventured then to ask her why
She thought she shook this way.
"I'm being followed by a man,
Whose dark cast dogs my days;
I am though safe inside the house –
You have saved me from his gaze".

'My dear, I'm glad to serve your case,
But still not clear to me,
Is how your dice will help to solve
This outlandish mystery.
Would you perchance elucidate,
In hope that you might yet be free?'

"Oh, dear sir, I will indeed,
My heart leaps at this chance;
I'd gladly give my toes or teeth,
To shun this monster's glance.
I cannot tell which way to go:
To Scotland, Holland, Wales or France."

"Hence the dice of which you speak,
I toss three at a time;
According to the added score,
Unless of course it should be prime,
I run towards the place they tell,
Until my feet are sore in grime."

"But 'tis all to no avail,
Even with disguise of green,
The tyrant's breath is always close,
His grey shade clearly seen;
It seems I can't escape his grasp,
And so can never feel serene."

"Until the sun takes rest at dusk,
There's only peace on Mars,
So in the creeping twilight
That precedes the birth of stars,
I wait, and watch the world go black
Then dread to see day break in bars."

"As in the ebony after-dark,
I am held in loving arms:
Invisible, invincible,
I know old Satan's charms,
But my respite at night's curtailed,
Since the red dawn never calms."

I listened carefully to her song,
And drew a diagram;
Was it clear or was it not?
Should I take a tot or dram?
'Dear friend,' I started, in high hope,
'Do you recognise this man?'

"Not really, but I know he's there,
His umber grizzled grey,
And no matter what I say or do,
He never ebbs away;
Somehow attached is he to me,
As is a pigeon to its clay."

'Clay, you say – how blind, how dim;
How my wits have done me down!
But now you've spoken at such length,
The line that joins the dots I've found:
It's clay that makes up your two feet –
Clay – not grime, that makes them brown.'

"Two feet of clay – by night or day
They have never come to mind,
But now you mention them I know
There's a portent in their kind;
I pray that you would now consent
To tell the meaning of this sign."

'I have to say, a misty cloud
Till now obscured the facts,
Yet now I hope to penetrate
The beast that breaks our backs.
May I surmise: your state of mind
Means you never will relax.'

'But now the fog fades from my view,
And crystal clear my window;
I have to say my doubts are few
Why you shake as wind shakes willow:
Your tremor's caused because you live
In mortal fear of your own shadow.'

YOUR MONEY OR YOUR LIFE

Put your money on the nail,
You're renting by the day;
You know the price will make you pale,
But there is no other way.

I am the Reaper, as you know,
Though a while you may survive,
But pay today or you must go;
You'll not escape this world alive.

How sad you can't keep me at bay,
To save yourself and wife,
You'd keep dusty death away,
With 'money for your life'.

But you'll become too ancient,
A worn-out shaking wreck –
Too old to raise your hand to write,
To sign the bloody cheque!

ALIENS

They walk among us at the dawn,
And also at the dusk;
They drift across our daily paths
And run the gauntlet of our scorn:
It seems to us they're human husks.

In city streets or in green fields
You'll find them on the prowl,
And if you should as much as look
Them in the eye without a shield,
They may reward you with a scowl.

On wheels or foot they ply their trade;
It's shameful what they do.
Is there no justice in this world
To free us from the games they've played,
So we can flourish, straight and true?

Some godly law of nine good points
Has no doubt been applied,
But by whose holy order is
It right to make our lives disjoint,
In placing peril on our side?

But open your eyes and breathe again;
Cast them up; regard the steeple –
As each soul comes in time ordained,
Some sublime and some insane,
All are simply – other people.

DESCARTES' SISTER

My brother René's famous now,
But no fame of any kind
Has ever settled on my head,
Yet scarcely do I mind.

After all he's droll and odd –
His musings rather rare
I'd say: more likely thought by God –
I doubt my path lies there.
His ideas are not complex
For me to understand
I think, but I shall seek
Another way to turn my whitened hand,
And your noble head maybe –
Far from the wailings at the wall
And arcane philosophy –
For recognition, and the call
To greatness that surely waits for me.
But would you put my mind at rest
To banish raging doubts that test
At certain times my sanity:

Observe me in the gilded mirror,
Above that side of ham;
Am I the fairest girl in France?
I do believe I am.

*It may not be immediately obvious, but the reader may
care to note that I am admired not only for my
breathtaking beauty, but also for my blushing modesty.*

THE TIME WILL COME

The time will come, so very soon,
Though hard to say how long,
When we'll be living on the moon;
Where did we all go wrong?

There's not much air up there you know,
And hard to grow your veg,
But there is one place you need not go –
That's out to cut your hedge.

Advantages? There's quite a dearth;
I'd rather be at home.
It's truly sad we wrecked this earth
And broke my garden gnome.

Even so, we must be strong,
Though wind and waves are high;
Just keep your nerve and come along –
It's really do or die.

Climb aboard the rocket ship
To say goodbye is hard;
Anyway, we must be off –
Just bring the pack of cards!

*I know how irritating it is to read the above, but
that's perhaps the whole point. After all, as you may
legitimately ask – how does an oyster make a pearl?*

A DEPRESSED OCTOPUS

I chanced across an octopus
In a sad and sorry state;
Aquiver were his tentacles,
Which might have made him late,
But otherwise they worked quite well
As far as I could fairly tell –
And he did at least have eight!

I felt I should enquire of him,
Or her – it was so hard to say,
If all his world was going well –
(He *was* prematurely grey).
The answer that he made to me,
Filtered up from swirling sea
As grim as Biscay Bay.

'Oh, woe is me this doleful day'
Rose in bubbles from the deep;
'Oh tell me where there's peace of mind,
Where I can have a hope of sleep.
The truth is that I've suffered so –
My life – in tatters – seems "de trop";
I'm just a wet and brownish heap!'

I took in pain this grave account,
Which caused me much concern,
And wondered if I'd heard the truth,
The way things really were;
(I will confess my "octo" isn't
What you'd really call proficient,
As it is quite hard to learn).

A language based in part on signs
From tentacles well drilled,
As well as on soft sounds submerged
That vex the hearer's skill,
Will always pose a supreme test:
Like taking off an old string vest
While drinking tea without a spill.

Though I was lost in reverie,
He just ploughed on in darker tones:
'My nature's sensitive you see,
Perhaps because I have no bones,
But even though I am of age,
Some insults make me boil and rage
And make my innards gripe and groan.'

'My instinct's that of one quite rare,
With insights few could rightly claim;
My sense of humour's quite sublime,
So how could "common" be my name?
And yet today I met a catfish
That dubbed me "Octopus vulgaris".
The manners of today I blame!'

I could see his point was made,
And yet there was no need to fret;
I would gladly give advice –
So little cause for such regret;
My counsel I was quick to state:
"Your legs are strong, so stand up straight,
Then light a Russian cigarette!"

The reader may note that 'Octopus vulgaris' is the usual name for a normal octopus, though I don't think the octopus appreciated it. The catfish was better educated than the octopus realised. Oh, the irony!

IF ONLY

When first we knew of it, we thought
The end had come at last;
A huge and hairy winged insect
Arrived, though with no blast of brass.
A vicious tint of red it was,
As though it had sucked dry of blood
All other creatures in its path –
Some in full flower, some in tiny bud.

Its wings and legs were veined with power,
With mandibles a match
For any soul who chanced nearby
Who thought he might just make a catch.
'Twas then this monstrous insect struck,
And plunged its high-powered steely sting
Into its victim's butter-flesh –
A clamour of internal bells to ring.

And then the thrashing insect flew
Straight up, in blaze of red,
Not ever to be seen again,
Except by others in pure dread,
Who'd hoped escape might be in sight;
But no such thing appeared to them,
As all were counted, head by head,
Whereupon the scourge had touched all men.

All that was fifty years ago –
I was a child at school,
But from that time, it's clear to me
A broom did sweep the earth by rule,
And banished evil, almost all,
Restored the good we had before,
Returned the climate as of old,
And now our human kindness strains no more.

We must tell those yet to come –
The children in our wombs,
Of our distress those years ago –
Of how our minds have many rooms,
And yet how some are missing;
Of how the world was once so mad
To trust its course to cunning rogues,
Whose ways were for the most part truly bad.

We have no wish to see again
The insect with that sting,
Though clear to us it took no blood,
But pumped a potion from its wings
That altered humans' views on things
And changed perception in a trice,
In order to relieve the sin;
To make, in time, each person much more wise.

The question that is hard to solve
Of course, is how it came.
My estimation of the truth,
In doubt, I offer all the same:
This world, that forever turns in hope,
Keeps for itself a piece of perfect gold;
A secret part, never to be breached,
No matter what should pass, nor ever what is told.

THE PRESCRIPTION

An apple a day
Keeps the doctor away,
As surely we all know so well;
But how to convey it,
And know he's received it,
Without actually ringing his bell?

You should use a strong box,
For a shiny ripe Cox,
Though if it is going by mail,
Make sure that you wrap it
In tissue and send it,
As soon as you can, without fail.

For a Beauty of Bath –
No really, don't laugh,
An ad in the paper is best;
Give a place to collect it,
And next day repeat it;
He can smuggle them out in his vest.

A Pink Lady is nice,
And not a bad price,
In seductive colours to boot;
Your doctor will love it,
With its flesh hypodermic –
It is such a superior fruit!

He won't want a cooker,
Though it is quite a looker,
Magnificent, weighty and green;
But a doctor will want it
Fairly sweet, or resent it,
Or say it's not good for his spleen.

For the busy GP,
Send a few more than three,
At long as the funds can be found.
'Consume the same day',
Is preferred, I would say;
It helps if your doctor's housebound!

One thing I must say,
You must heed right away –
It's to do with maggots and bugs:
Your apple – do clean it,
So your doctor won't see it
Was once a nice rest home for slugs!

If you play your cards right,
You'll secure without fight,
An absence of medical strife;
Or you'll have to submit,
And dark probings permit –
Either that, or just run for your life!

CANARY ISLANDS

The Canary Isles
Have few crocodiles,
Which is good, I think you'll agree,
But without mincing words,
They're bursting with birds,
In red, blue, purple and green.

Namely pigeons and swifts
That haunt the dark cliffs,
But sometimes sit quietly in trees –
And bustards and choughs,
Though that's not enough:
There are chiffchaffs and chats, if you please!

And yet other birds,
All feathered, not furred –
You know the ones that I mean?
They're canaries of course,
As yellow as gorse,
And all around here to be seen.

It's their name that is odd;
It comes not from God,
But from their islands of birth,
Which were named, it's no lie:
Canariae Insulae,
By Romans with no sense of mirth!

It's maybe a rumour
They lacked such good humour,
But one thing we surely can say:
That birds in the trees
They left to their ease,
But couldn't stand growling all day.

For the isles were beset
With one kind of pet,
With names such as Fido and Rover:
Large dogs and small,
Held the island in thrall,
As they barked all day, over and over.

Hence the name of today,
Though the dogs swam away,
And barked somewhere else unrestrained;
At least the birds stayed,
And chirruped away,
So the isles are at peace once again.

Readers no doubt have their own theories about how the name of the Canary Islands originated, but it is interesting to see the coat of arms of the said islands, which clearly depicts two large dogs with collars, (but no leads!), supporting a shield. The other thing of course is that 'canis' is the Latin term for 'dog'.

We have our own 'Canary Island' in Britain. It is called The Isle of Dogs, in central London. There are probably plenty of dogs there, but not many canaries, except perhaps for the odd one in a cage. However, it is remarkable that Canary Wharf lies at the northern boundary of the Isle of Dogs, isn't it?

A LIFE AT SEA

From time to time, my cousin Prue,
In worry that the world fell short,
Found men to prate and strut and snort
And fail to be of good report;
Such anguish was her residue.

Her other trial, her pale green skin –
'Genetic fluke', the doctors said –
Was ever present, save in bed,
Where she could cover hands and head
And conjure dreams of better things.

How wild, how free, the ocean seemed,
Untamed, unknown – a vast expanse
Of green that called to Prue – romance!
In time her feelings grew intense,
And drew her nearer to her dream.

The swelling wave with noble crest
That crashed with thunder on the shore;
The sun that rose to light the dawn
And give its life to those unborn –
Were forces Prue could not resist.

Beneath the waves a silent world
Was lit in green by filtered light –
But then loomed up within her sight,
A soundless orchestra, which quite
Shook Prue, who uttered not a word.

In her mind, she saw herself:
A belle, a mermaid at the neap
And spring – and angel of the keep;
Queen of all creatures of the deep,
And preening on a coastal shelf.

The undulating tubes and fronds,
Conducted by an octopus,
Seemed to say: 'Now come to us,
We waited patient years in trust
That you'd appear – pray give response'.

Delighted by this overture,
The octopus and Prue entwined,
And danced around a rock combined.
"Oh, yes my darling – how sublime,
I'll stay forever, that is sure!"

"The love you have is manifest;
At last I feel that all is right
And even if with all my might,
Resist this aqueous delight,
My heart knows that here I'll find my rest".

The octopus then made reply:
'My name is Sue, and I must say –
That happiness has found its way
To our ladies' secret hideaway'.
With that, she smiled and gave a sigh.

So it was that Prue had chanced
To find an underwater home,
Far beneath the crash of foam;
She'd justified her yen to roam –
A lady clearly quite entranced!

"I'm in thrall; I do so like
Your ladies' paradise that's here;
I did enjoy our dance, it's clear,
But might I ask one question, dear?
Is there an octopus called Mike?"

THE VOICE IN THE BOX

Always present, never there,
They cannot quite be understood;
The listener marvels at the words
Emerging from the varnished wood –
Or indeed whatever's there,
To send the message through the air.

But notice that the spoken sounds
Are shifting shapes that seem to soothe;
They're so erotic, yet hypnotic,
The strains emerging from the booth.
The truth is rarer than hens' teeth,
As they have banished unbelief.

Who was that lady speaking then?
Is she human, from this earth?
She says she's going to be your friend,
But hard to judge her claim to worth.
She's going to write your message down,
And keep it safely, never frown.

But do take care, I urge you now,
Unbridled charms she will release;
You have no proof she's on your side,
No reason for your pains to ease.
If I were you, I'd humour her,
And give due pause: somehow demur.

I've met this circumstance before;
In innocence I gave my all,
My message given out in full,
Too late to hesitate or stall.
She had it all down on a disc,
Which placed me with a fearsome risk.

Taken from a dreamless sleep,
Though flight of angels it was not –
Descending through the violet haze,
To a vile and bleak and brackish spot;
In my sky now sail two moons,
And underfoot, red sandy dunes.

But truth to tell, I wish it were
So different – that I had been strong;
My temptress lured me to the rocks,
A Siren calling in full song –
And now I live but half a life,
Little more than stress and strife.

No need to suffer as I did,
Just ignore those calls to speak;
I'm far away – there's no return,
Just be strong, and wait a week,
Or you risk a heart infarction –
If work you must for those damned Martians.

ONE HOUR

If a man, with all his lifelong sin,
Did find his final hour had surely come,
How could he spend it better than begin
His journey to the other side struck dumb,
But listening, though with happy halted tongue,
To the solace that Rachmaninov might bring?

There can for certain be no finer way,
To live one's last hour in this sullied world,
And know this special man, now veiled in grey,
Went once his own way, as his soul unfurled,
His time best spent on earth creating gold,
In certain proof that alchemy held sway.

For this very man himself one day came down,
From on high, but with no trumpet blare,
For him, his earthly toil 'sine qua non':
To crystallise pure beauty by his care.
Within a thousand years, this world may drown,
Yet Sergei's art will ever hold the crown.

WHILE WE LIVE

Before you're born
You don't exist,
At least, you would think so,
But then you suddenly arrive,
In a pink and noisy glow.

Now you're here
You just stay put,
And live your life right through,
And all the time you're here with us,
You're only one, not two.

You'll think me
Rather mad I know,
But that's the risk I'll run:
If you can make one from just none,
Then why not two from one?

Though yes, it's true,
That's rhetoric,
And commonplace to see:
If you're one already then
One more you cannot be.

And when you're gone,
It seems the end,
But do not be so sure;
You're back to none again my friend –
You've opened up the door!

IT CAME

In late August, when sweet summer's
Final breaths were close,
It came; in the cool and calm of night
One eve that told perhaps of hope ahead,
When some who'd lived but now were dead,
Perforce accepted stillness, yet were unquiet.

It came, perhaps to bring to mind
The ever onward-going
Mystery this life entails;
To say somehow there is another place,
Not in our normal time, nor of our space,
And far beyond the human mental scale.

Whatever is the case, it came –
As a silver coin, above
The metal curtain rail,
Whereupon, in one smooth swoop it fell,
In perverse, reverse J-shape to tell,
In coded language, something of its tale.

It came to this good earth with sound,
Upon a wooden desk;
A fevered search then met with no success.
This coin, from a world unknown
To humans bred of blood and bone,
Had there returned, to frozen timelessness.

*The above tells of events which occurred in the very early
hours of August 26th 1998 at a house in West Street, Shoreham by Sea, West Sussex, following the death of the author's
mother six days earlier. No explanation has ever been found.*

BENT TO THE WIND

My uncle seldom used a walking-stick,
Despite the cumulative gravity
Of the years, that bent his groaning frame
Into no more than mere cavities
Formed of the skin and bone that he became.

Covered now by a dishevelled old coat,
And dragging ragged trousers in the dust,
He made his uncertain way past the trees
Fringing the duckpond, and it seemed a gust
Or breeze would bring him to his knees.

But not so; somehow his ancient pinstripes,
Flapping in unexpected unison,
Endowed him with the wisdom of the wind –
Gave raison d'être: the strength to carry on,
And rise above his catalogue of sins.

He never noticed inconvenience,
Just carried on as though 'twere all the same;
His journey to the lane was hardly quick,
As yes, it was windy, but was he to blame?
No indeed, so why should he use a stick?

Such logic crushed mere mortals at a stroke,
But uncle never was quite of their ilk;
Long years ago a comet spanned the sky,
And told of his arrival on blue silk –
Which could not speak in words, so did not lie.

And from this notable inception came
The man of paradox we knew those days,
His lodestar tuned by inner gyroscope,
Which was itself empowered by DNA –
Therefore no need to wonder, care or hope.

When the wind dropped a little he went on,
And by degrees attained the old gatepost
At the end of the garden by the lane.
Determination was what mattered most,
Despite the thorns and thistles in your way.

And there, he had a little time to wait,
While the wind waned and found new directions.
No need now for the wind; it was the end
Of the journey; no need now for corrections –
No time to find another fence to mend.

Soon enough the colour ebbed from the sky,
And a crescented moon appeared with the stars.
Not far down the wintry lane was a bend,
Round which came in silence a huge black car.
He sat inside; he was never seen again.

ABOUT US

DICK DIXON

Dick Dixon was born in Sawbridgeworth, Hertfordshire; he works as a teacher at a college on the south coast of England. While at school, he won the Ilott prize for poetry in 1962. He graduated in mathematics in 1970 from the University of Wales, as it was then, and embarked on a rather chequered career, involving an insurance company, a British Rail drawing office, and various other ventures.

Eventually, light appeared at the end of the tunnel, and he realised that the answer surely was to engage in the teaching of mathematics (though the precise nature of the question has remained obscure).

Some time ago, in 2013, he met Reine Mazoyer, the French artist, and it became quite clear quite quickly that together, they would have to write their book 'Rhymes for no Reason', after which it seemed churlish not to continue with 'The Rimes of the Newfangled Mariner', and the 'The Curse of The Square Crow', the present volume. In this book we hope you will be able to detect something of interest, or find a little something to amuse you when the cold inhospitable world has failed to come up with the goods!

REINE MAZOYER

Reine Mazoyer is a French artist. She was born in Montbrison in southern France and graduated from the 'Ecole des Beaux-Arts' at Saint-Etienne in 1965.

She married Robert Mazoyer (who died in 1999), the well-known movie-film director, and worked with him as art director. Later she worked as a director for documentary movies. She exhibits her art creations regularly in Europe and the United States.

Reine received the honour of 'Chevalier des Arts et des Lettres' in 2008.

After having written and illustrated two books herself, Reine met Dick Dixon, and they realised that they were definitely crazy enough to create more books together! Reine has now illustrated three books in this series: 'Rhymes for no Reason', 'The Rimes of the Newfangled Mariner', and now the current book 'The Curse of The Square Crow'. There will most probably be more to come!

Dick Dixon and Reine Mazoyer at the Book Stop Café
in Eymet, France, in July 2016.

The author's niece Lucy with her birthday copy of
The Rimes of the Newfangled Mariner

The original Square Crow, as constructed
by Reine Mazoyer

Et maintenant, voici une introduction aux poèmes en Français.

Le Corbeau Carré

Oh Mon Dieu... voilà une bien triste histoire!

Le brave Corbeau Carré est certainement un oiseau, mais il ne ressemble à aucun autre. Il est constitué de cubes étranges qui lui interdisent de vivre comme tout bon oiseau qui se respecte.

Il lui est très difficile de voler ou même marcher, et jouer au cricket est hors de question, même avec des pattes carrées!

Pour lui, le seul moyen d'arriver à circuler est de s'asseoir sur le toit d' un autobus, ou d' un taxi, en espérant qu'il ira dans la bonne direction!

Evidemment – vous avez deviné je suppose – le pire, pour un corbeau carré, est de pondre des œufs, du moins pour Madame Corbeau Carré...

Ouille! Pauvre petite!

La Photo

Une vieille photo de famille oubliée depuis longtemps, a surgit, cachée derrière une porte coulissante.

Que de souvenirs! Cousins, tantes, oncles, toute cette foule de membres de «la famille» qui vous entourent, petit enfant, au moment des vacances... il y a si longtemps...

Ainsi que la photo l'illustre, ils aimaient les plages dorées, le soleil, manger et boire ensemble et toutes sortes d'autres festivités dont je me sentais exclu.

Qui étaient ces gens? Que pensaient-ils? Cela n'avait pas d' importance pour eux...Vous pouvez le pensez et je le dis!

Quelle bonne idée si je pouvais prendre ma revanche sur ces animaux sans cœur...

La seule façon raisonnable de trouver la paix et une juste revanche, après tout ce temps, serait de brûler la photo, de détruire toute trace de ces horribles personnes dans mon univers... bien fait pour eux!

Ahhh, je me sens mieux!

L' Amour des Haricots

Bon, que se passe-t-il? Pourquoi ces haricots sont-ils en train de sauter? C' est peut-être le Printemps qui les rends si joyeux?

Pas vraiment – ce sont des haricots sauteurs Mexicains et j'ai bien peur qu'il n'y ait qu'une réponse à cette énigme... je pense qu'ils sont un peu «en manque».

Ce n'est pas facile de trouver votre partenaire quand vous êtes coincés dans une coque sombre et chaude, c'est sans doute très frustrant, je pense.

Mais ces gars sont déterminés, et pas du tout «has been» si vous voyez ce que je veux dire!

J'espère qu'ils vont réussir et être capable de repeupler Mexico et peut-être d'autres parties du monde.

Maintenant, je suis certain que vous réalisez qu'il y a un risque de disparition de ces haricots, causé par leur difficulté à se reproduire.

Malheureusement, nous ne voyons pas souvent ces haricots amoureux en Grande Bretagne.

Ils n'aiment sans doute pas la froid et la pluie.

Néanmoins, nous avons des haricots sur nos toasts!

Le Blues

Bon... c'est ainsi. Oui, chaque jour me rappelle mon enfance et mes tentatives infructueuses pour apprendre à jouer correctement du piano. Le gros piano noir est toujours là, dans la «salle de musique» - pas terrible, ce nom - et il me hante! Je veux seulement vivre ma vie et oublier ce terrible problème!

Quand je pense au temps que j'ai passé à faire des gammes en faisant un bruit épouvantable, je m'étonne de ne pas avoir encore reçu la visite de la police, mais je suppose qu'ils ont mieux à faire, par exemple empêcher les gens de jouer du violon ou du tuba.

Peu importe, vous ne serez pas surpris de découvrir que le pire est à venir. Comment vous sentiriez vous si, un jour, en descendant l'escalier, vous pouviez entendre une merveilleuse mélodie jouée par quelqu'un qui s'appelle Tibbles, détalant sur les touches du piano. Oui, c'est vrai, jouée par un chat - qui n'avait même pas pris de leçons de piano!

Déprimant!

Dans la Soupe

Voilà une histoire extraordinaire, une innovation capitale dans les concours de cuisine.

Tout le monde a vu ces concours de cuisine à la télévision, il y en a toujours un, à n'importe quel moment.

Tandis que vous perdez votre temps en lisant cela, vous pourriez gagner le premier prix pour le meilleur soufflé en France, ou peut-être dans le monde, après tout!

Cependant, il s'agit ici d'une cuisine différente. Ce concours demande beaucoup de soin, une totale dévotion, et des qualités personnelles difficiles à trouver de nos jours, peut-être jamais. Mais il n'existe aucun autre concours semblable à celui-ci, je vous l'assure, il est vraiment unique.

Le prix est la célébrité, et le gagnant sera honoré et même célébré durant les décades à venir.

Si vous voulez vraiment gagner le concours: «le plat de l' année», vous devez être vous- même «le plat».

Vous serez parfaitement cuit dans une grande marmite, avec la quantité nécessaire d'herbes appropriées, pendant le temps recommandé, avec tous les égards qui vous sont dû. A la suite de quoi, vous serez éternellement adoré.

Découverte!

Cette histoire démontre comment des évènements du présent peuvent mettre en lumière (et en chaleur!) les évènements du passé (lointain).

Comment pensez-vous que le feu a été découvert? Il existe beaucoup d'explications, ici et là: le contact de métaux entre eux créant des étincelles, un procédé incroyablement difficile à mettre en œuvre en frottant des surfaces ensemble pour les chauffer jusqu' à ce qu'elles brûlent. Il paraît que c'est possible et je me souviens de mon grand-père me racontant qu'il avait vu un très vieil homme fatigué commencer de faire du feu de cette manière en Afrique du Sud, pendant la première guerre mondiale. Mais, vraiment, qui pensez-vous peut avoir le courage et l'énergie de faire çà? Cet homme avait sans doute seulement vingt-cinq ans.

Non, la seule façon de faire du feu a été découverte il y a mille ans. Une jeune femme venait juste de laver ses sous-vêtements, peut-être dans un torrent, puis a essayé de les faire sécher en les suspendant dans un buisson un jour de canicule, et, évidemment, ils ont pris feu!

Vous pouvez parier qu'elle ne l'a pas fait deux fois!

Déshabillage

Tout le monde connaît les lundis matin. Ce sont de terribles expériences dans le monde entier. Beaucoup d'entre nous sont sortis d'un lit bien chaud pour mettre des vêtements bizarres et inconfortables puis sont allés dans le froid et l'humidité seulement pour faire un travail complètement inutile. Cela ne vous semble pas ridicule? Subir ce stress pour aller travailler – comme ils disent-tous assis en rangs, tapant toute la matinée sur un clavier qui ne marche pas bien. Comment peuvent-ils appeler ça vivre!

Oh, si seulement vendredi pouvait arriver plus vite, nous pourrions nous déshabiller et peut être aller plus loin et participer à une «orgie» au cinquième étage (hors de la vue des managers). Donnez-nous du heavy métal, de l'alcool et de la coke et nous pourrons nous débarrasser de nos frustrations – et plus besoin de vêtements non plus!

Mais, si, au réveil, nous découvrons que nous avons rêvé – quel cauchemar!

Cinq par Jour

Je me sens assez concerné par les fruits et les légumes. Nous entendons tout le temps dire qu'il faut consommer au moins cinq de ces ennuyeuses choses chaque jour! OK, certaines ne sont pas mal je suppose, mais que pensez-vous des épinards et des courgettes, ou des groseilles à maquereaux? Votre corps tout entier ne tremble-t-il pas à l'idée de sentir ces monstruosités descendre dans votre gosier, jusqu' aux endroits les plus profonds? OK, certains peuvent aimer ça, les Martiens peut-être?

Bon, pensez ce que vous voulez, si vous n'avez pas vos «cinq par jour», vous courez le risque de ne plus être de ce monde dans longtemps. En fait, je ne serai pas surpris de découvrir qu'il s'agit d'un complot fomenté par les légumes pour pénétrer dans l'estomac des êtres humains! Malins ces légumes non?

Cela me parait injuste, car les chiens, les chats et même les souris semblent avoir été exemptés et peuvent mâcher sans soucis des os, du poisson et du fromage!

Mais il y a le revers de la médaille, vous devez faire attention à ne pas exagérer, vous pouvez sans doute manger cinq pépins de courges sans problème, mais vous ne pouvez pas manger la courge tout entière! Cela ne compterait que pour un! Quel soulagement, hein?

Cirque Crocodile

Bon, voici une étrange expérience de vie. Je dois admettre qu'il est surréaliste de rencontrer un crocodile dans la rue et exceptionnel un crocodile fait de sacs à mains en cuir rouge!

Ce crocodile était très amical et probablement très bien élevé et avait eu une vie passionnante. Je l'ai trouvé fascinant dès le début et nous avons conversé ensemble de toutes sortes de choses.

Je suis un incorrigible curieux, je ne pouvais pas m'empêcher de chercher ce que l'on pourrait appeler «le crocodile dans la chambre» (en référence à une expression Anglaise: «un éléphant dans la chambre». Cette question était: est-il fait du même cuir dedans et dehors? Voici un cas resté inconnu de la science médicale, je pense.

A mon grand plaisir, il m'a permis de de faire un simple test pour découvrir sa «nature intérieure». Il m'a confié ne pas très bien la connaître lui-même et qu'il serait heureux de satisfaire sa curiosité.

J'ai donc tenté l'expérience d'introduire mon bras entre ses dents aiguisées, jusque dans sa gorge, pour voir ce que je pourrais bien y trouver.

A mon grand étonnement, c'était du cuir de sac à main rouge tout le long, et pas seulement, car, en prime, j'ai pu remonter des profondeurs un petit miroir, du mascara, un tube de rouge à lèvres et un peigne!

Combien de temps?

Vous savez ce que c'est que d'attendre l'autobus. Tandis que le temps passe, vous faites peu à peu partie d'un décor différent qui devient, au fur et à mesure que vous attendez, une autre réalité. Tous les éléments et forces de la nature sont altérés et se transforment, comme dans un rêve, d'une façon inattendue, inhabituelle. Vous êtes ailleurs, dans un autre espace-temps. Peut- être êtes-vous quelqu'un d'autre? Le soleil, la lune, le ciel, la mer et le paysage jouent tous un double jeux. Cela peut être une aventure, mais cela peut être aussi inquiétant.

Qui a besoin de prendre l'autobus, vous demandez vous? Quand l'autobus arrive, vous pouvez être surpris et même avoir oublié votre destination.

Etes-vous certain de vouloir aller quelque part? Ne préféreriez-vous pas mieux être dans un désert hanté, quand les fleurs s'épanouissent à l'aube? Ou chevaucher sur une plage au crépuscule, chanter avec les dauphins sous la mer?

Voulez-vous vraiment rentrer chez vous et faire une tasse de thé? Vous n'en savez rien, je pense. N'est-ce pas justement ça la vie?

Alors, bonne chance – et puis zut! l'autobus est passé, mais vous l' avez manqué. Maintenant c'est votre dernière chance!

Le Paradis sur Terre

Ceci est peut-être une triste histoire, mais aussi un célébration de la beauté de l'imagination et une reconnaissance de notre besoin de voir les choses autrement que ce qu'elles paraissent être. Nous souhaitons, nous espérons, mais y at-il une réponse?

Quand j'avais sept ans dans les années 50, quelque chose d'impossible à croire pour moi maintenant est arrivé. Une douce petite fille, Gillian, dans ma classe à l'école primaire, est subitement tombée malade et a été emmenée à l'hôpital. Elle a eu une opération de l'appendicite en urgence mais a décédé tragiquement. Je savais que tout le monde devait mourir un jour, mais cela me semblait terriblement injuste.

Je pense quelquefois à ce triste événement et me souviens combien j'étais choqué car c'était ma première expérience de la mort.

Serait-il possible qu'elle soit encore là, avec moi, juste pour une journée?

J'aimerais bien.

La vie est-elle une question sans réponse?

La mort est-elle une réponse sans question?

Lamentations du Morse

Vous savez ce que c'est d'être bloqué dans un endroit inconnu, hostile et peut-être dangereux. Un cloporte a t'il vraiment envie de vivre dans une bûche de bois humide et un perce oreille désire-t-il vraiment installer son logement dans un morceau de fruit pourri? Quel projet!

Ils préfèrent certainement être dans une maison et s'amuser sur un tapis bien chaud!

Et bien c'est pareil pour un morse, je pense. Le pauvre animal obligé de vivre dans les espaces gelés de l'Arctique doit attraper ses propres poissons et trouver un endroit à peu près confortable comme maison. Est-ce possible ou même raisonnable? Il lui a poussé de longues défenses en signe de protestation, sans aucun doute!

Il préfère certainement être dans un zoo chaud, amical et hospitalier où des poissons goûteux lui sont distribués à 4 heures de l'après -midi précises chaque jour de la semaine et où il peut avoir d'intéressantes conversations avec ses amis. C'est ce que veut ce morse, c'est sûr! Il a dû trouver des informations sur le zoo par internet. La vie moderne hein?

Le Dilemme

Prue était ma cousine préférée. J'avais toujours admiré son courage, sa détermination et son sens de l'humour, associé à une nature douce et sensible. En même temps, elle était aussi très attirante, si vous voyez ce que je veux dire. Il avait seulement un petit quelque-chose qu'elle avait reçu à sa naissance. Personne ne savait pourquoi ni comment mais c'était ainsi: sa peau avait, sans aucun doute, une étrange couleur verdâtre. Cela lui avait toujours causé des problèmes dans la vie. Comme ses docteurs étaient impuissants, elle avait résolu de prendre la situation en mains. La meilleure solution, pensait-elle, serait de laisser la nature résoudre par elle-même ce problème, par exemple, en se faisant bronzer au soleil.

C'est pourquoi Prue décida de rendre visite à un camps de nudistes en plein été, quand le soleil serait assez fort pour donner une autre couleur à sa peau et sans doute éliminer les vilains reflets verts qui avaient gâchés toutes sa vie.

L'histoire raconte son voyage à «Sunnyside» et comment elle avait quitté tous ses vêtements dans sa chambre pour rejoindre les autres invités, célébrant une fête d' anniversaire avec du champagne. Cela a été très réconfortant pour elle de découvrir qu'elle n'était pas la seule à avoir ce problème: il était clair que les autres invités avaient aussi la peau verte!

Le Pendule

Oh, cher lecteur! Voilà une terrible histoire et un avertissement pour nous tous!

C'est très désagréable pour la victime, mais je dois dire que ce genre de chose a dû arriver plusieurs fois dans le passé, aussi embarrassant que ce soit.

Imaginez comment un jeune gars comme vous doit se sentir après avoir passé de nombreuses minutes avec sa fiancée pour planifier son mariage, depuis l'uniforme des serveuses jusqu'aux verres pour la réception et des milliers d'autres choses bien sûr. Tout cela a dû être méticuleusement préparé en avance, naturellement. Et quand le grand jour arrive, les deux vont devenir vraiment Mari et Femme.

Il y a une chose qui n'a pas été planifiée dans cette cérémonie à laquelle vous allez participer. Si vous n'avez pas été assez méticuleux ou avez bu un peu trop de «jus de raisin» (ou un breuvage similaire) que ce passe-t-il si votre «garçon d'honneur» qui vous a mis au lit pour être prêt pour le grand jour, que ce passe-t-il si votre garçon d' honneur a trouvé votre fiancée à son goût, tellement à son goût qu' il n'a pas pu s'empêcher de vous attacher les jambes avec une longue corde et a fixé l' autre bout de la corde au sommet d'une cheminée?

Alors quoi, hein? Plus de mariage, j'en ai peur, tandis-que le traître s'enfuit de l'autre coté de la colline avec votre fiancée! Quelle horrible femme! Il vaut sans doute mieux que vous restiez loin d'elle de toute façon!

Un Nouveau Calendrier

Oh, fantastique! Imaginez combien il serait merveilleux d'avoir des étés plus longs et des hivers plus courts. La punition d'avoir à supporter de vivre décembre, janvier et février pourrait être réduite à moins de neuf semaines. Plus besoin d'avoir peur de sortir le matin dans un paysage sombre et glacé et d'avoir à prendre une voiture couverte de six pieds de neige.

Tout ce qu'il faut, c'est donner vingt jours au lieu de trente à ces mois, simple!

Le printemps, c'est à dire mars, avril, arriverait plus tôt, mais nous n'avons pas encore atteint le meilleur, nous devons donc aussi leur donner un plus petit nombre de jours, je dirais vingt-cinq chacun. Nous pourrions profiter des jonquilles bercées par le vent, du gazouillis des oiseaux et des grouillements des petits animaux dans le sol, faisant ce qu'ils font d'habitude. Nous pourrions aussi nous habituer à voir nos champs remplis de moutons laineux – sans doute une partie du grand «plan» de la nature.

Puis nous avons le printemps tardif, soit mai et juin, prêts à nous donner les belles fleurs des jardins, les chants d'oiseaux et le va et vient incessant des tondeuses dévorant une herbe bourgeonnante prête à envahir la maison tout entière si elle le pouvait. Il y aura aussi un grand remue-ménage derrière les buissons, causé la plus part du temps par des activités entre humains qui sont particulièrement nombreuses à cette période de l'année, accompagnées de sons mélodieux qui embellissent en général ce type de cérémonies. Oh, cher lecteur, comme vous aimeriez découvrir ces activités!

Pour laisser du temps à tous ces merveilleux évènements du printemps tardif, nous avons besoin d'au moins onze semaines, non?

Enfin voici le bel été – juillet, août et septembre, quand toutes nos inhibitions pourront enfin s'envoler et que nous pourrons batifoler sans retenue sur des plages sans limites, dépensant notre vitalité sans compter, nos corps huilés pour recevoir un soleil glorieux. Il y aura, évidemment encore du remue- ménage, mais je pense cette fois-ci, plutôt derrière un rocher approprié. A ce moment- là vous pourrez probablement remarquer l'utilité des algues, comme une sorte de feuille de figuier.

Aucun doute, c'est notre période préférée et nous avons besoin de dix-sept semaines pour elle, Youpee!

Mais hélas, il y a toujours un prix à payer pour nos plaisirs. Nous devons nous préparer doucement aux horreurs de l'hiver. Encore que ce ne sera pas si mal maintenant, avec notre système, nous devons juste passer une période de pluie, brouillard et boue, de jours plus courts, et peut- être de mauvaise humeur. Environ huit semaines seront bien suffisantes, avant que nous ne nous sentions gelés!

Bon, je pense que nous avons fait quelque progrès ne pensez-vous pas, avec un long été et un court hiver? Pourquoi ne pas le faire?

Après tout, personne n'a jamais fait une omelette sans casser des œufs!

Une Nouvelle Race de Bouledogue

Ceci est une drôle d'histoire concernant l'évolution biologique, toujours d'actualité semble-t-il.

Prenez l'exemple d'une porcherie. Il y a un million d'années, le cochon était un animal très terrien. Si il avait sauté d'un haut building (il y a sans doute un petit million d' années!) le cochon se serait écrasé au sol, avec un drôle de bruit, plutôt que de s'envoler dans le vent. Aujourd'hui nous avons tous entendu parler des cochons volants. «Quand les cochons voleront, les poules auront des dents,» dit-on dans la conversation.

Il est difficile de savoir ce qui a fait que les cochons sont devenus capables de voler – peut-être un régime spécial, mais nous pouvons constater la même évolution chez les chiens, du moins chez les bouledogues. Il semble clair que cette évolution ne soit pas due au souhait de son créateur d'en faire un animal volant, pour attraper un petit oiseau au vol par exemple, au lieu de manger sa nourriture par terre? Non, c'est sûrement le régime du bouledogue.

Vous avez certainement remarqué que les bouledogues (et d'autres chiens aussi) aiment attraper les guêpes et les mouches – quoique je pense qu'ils préfèrent les guêpes – directement en vol et les manger avec délice. Ils semblent adorer cette activité, en dépit de son danger, mais c'est bien sûr programmé dans leur cerveau, sans que les bouledogues en soient conscients. Il y a certainement dans le corps de la guêpe une substance chimique qui produit des changements dans le corps du chien.

Si vous observez l'illustration, vous allez remarquer les petites ailes qui prennent forme et, clairement, dans le futur, le ciel va être peuplé de cochons et de bouledogues volants, se battant pour leur nourriture.

Le côté positif de cette nouvelle race de chiens est que vous n'aurez pas besoin d'aller les promener.

Nuits d'insomnie

Voici un homme toujours inquiet. Le monde ne va pas bien et c'est de pire en pire! Une vision vraiment pessimiste du futur l'envahi. Ce n'est donc pas surprenant qu'il n'arrive pas à dormir, et nous savons tous qu'il n'y a rien de mieux qu'une bonne nuit de sommeil. Il décide finalement d'essayer la vieille méthode du comptage des moutons – qui sont évidemment des moutons virtuels, car il est difficile d'en rencontrer au dernier étage d'un appartement en ville!

Il décide donc, avec espoir, de créer ses propres moutons virtuels en fermant les yeux, mais découvre qu'ils sont difficiles à contrôler. Ils sont partout, errants sans but, cherchant pense-t-il quelque nourriture imaginaire, il est impossible de les compter, particulièrement parce qu'ils se ressemblent tous!

Mais il a, dans son demi-sommeil, une idée. Il a fait décorer sa chambre récemment et les décorateurs ont laissé derrière eux un pot de peinture rouge. Le problème du comptage allait être résolu puisqu'il allait pouvoir marquer chaque mouton par un numéro à la peinture rouge.

Bon, c'était une bonne idée!

Une Situation Difficile

Le Langage peut-être un vrai problème!

Que se passerait-il si toutes les choses dont vous parlez, y compris les dinosaures, la gravité zéro ou les méduses et même si ces expressions courantes comme «Il pleut des cordes» ou «avoir un chat dans la gorge» ou «une mouche dans la pommade» se mettaient réellement à exister?

Je ne crois pas que j'ai jamais vu «une mouche dans la pommade» et j'aurais certainement libéré la pauvre chose de sa prison si je l'avais vue.

Néanmoins, cela peut exister et nous comprenons ce que cela veut dire.

Voici l' histoire d'une malheureuse mouche qui a découvert qu' elle avait été mise au monde par un créateur qui trouvait normal de rendre possible toutes les choses dont on parle. Naturellement, cette mouche dans la pommade aurait peut-être préféré cela plutôt que «il pleut des cordes» ou être «l'oiseau du matin attrapant le ver de terre»... mais pas le ver de terre!

La Malédiction des Tremblements

Voici une étrange histoire...Il y est question d'une femme atteinte d'un mal étrange, elle tremble de fièvre car elle pense être suivie par un homme monstrueux portant des vêtements sombres. Vous imaginez sa détresse! Elle se demande pourquoi cet homme ne parle jamais et elle n'a aucune idée de ce qu'il attend d'elle. Il la suit partout, toute la journée. La nuit elle retrouve un peu de tranquillité quand il disparait mais bien sûr, il revient chaque matin dans la même tenue que la veille.

Elle a cherché plusieurs moyens pour découvrir qui il était, y compris la vieille méthode du lancer de dés pour savoir où changer de direction, mais il trouvait toujours le moyen d'être là.

Ce cas était très inquiétant pour le docteur à qui elle avait confié son problème, jusqu'à ce qu'il remarque la couleur de ses pieds: la couleur de l'argile, étrange n'est-ce pas? Elle pensait que c'était à cause du sol qui avait donné, en marchant, cette couleur à ses pieds, mais un examen plus approfondi a révélé que ses pieds étaient réellement faits d'argile.

Alors, le docteur a immédiatement fait le rapprochement: les gens aux pieds d'argile ne sont pas très courageux, n'est-ce-pas? Nous en avons maintenant la preuve. Etre peureux ne veux pas dire que vous êtes une mauvaise personne!

Voilà l'explication: Chaque fois, c'était son ombre qui lui faisait peur! Peut-être avait-elle consulté le mauvais docteur!

De l'Argent pour Vivre

Quand une personne en bonne santé découvre que son temps sur terre arrive à sa fin, que fait-elle?

Cet homme a eu une idée. Un jour où tout allait mal, juste après le thé, La faucheuse, cousine de l'Ange de la Mort lui apparut, alors qu'il était assis dans son canapé, dans le salon.

Comme il était âgé et en mauvaise santé, il réalisa que La Faucheuse était venue pour lui prendre son âme. Au cas où il n'aurait pas compris, la faucheuse expliqua qu'elle devait toujours ajouter à sa collection et ne voulait pas manquer une chance de gagner des points de bonus pour accéder au poste de direction.

Néanmoins, l'homme pensa qu'il pouvait traiter un accord avec La Faucheuse, sous la forme d'une donation pour une bonne santé sur terre. La Faucheuse accepta cette possibilité à condition qu'il puisse payer par chèque au nom de G. Faucheuse Esq. Elle expliqua que la Direction prendrait ses dividendes plus tard.

Cela engagerait une somme considérable par an mais cet accord pourrait être annulé si l'homme devenait trop vieux et tremblant pour signer le chèque.

Alors, l'âme ferait partie de la collection, le lundi matin suivant.

Un accord semblable pourrait être pris avec sa femme, a fait remarquer la faucheuse, disant qu'elle reviendrait le lendemain.

Heureusement, l'homme était dans la cuisine en train de préparer des sandwiches et n'avait rien entendu.

Je ne sais pas ce qui s'est passé ensuite mais je suis sûr qu'ils sont tous morts joyeusement plus tard!

Les Autres

N'était-ce pas Jean Paul Sartre qui avait dit «L'enfer c'est les autres»? Peut-être ne saurons-nous jamais ce qu'il voulait dire exactement, mais je me souviens que trois personnes devaient rester ensemble le reste de leur vie dans une seule pièce. C'était une version de l'enfer, semble-t-il. Heureusement, pas d'huile bouillante ni de charbons ardents, quel soulagement!

Sans doute pensait-il à cette notion de «l'autre» que nous avons tous sans jamais comprendre vraiment ce que sont «les autres» êtres humains. Cela semble surprenant, mais pas impossible, car nous sommes tous des humains (si vous pouvez lire cela), si vous ne pouvez pas, pas de panique!

Qui sont les humains, et pourquoi sont-ce qu'ils sont? Difficile de répondre, pour moi en tout cas! Mais si vous pensez que c'est une question stupide, imaginez un avenir où un scientifique aurait créé un être qui marche, parle et fait les choses que les humains font, peut-être même a-t-il des cheveux blonds, des yeux bleus et la peau douce, sauf qu'il n'est pas certain que cette personne existe. Elle pourrait être crée par des algorithmes, ou par autre chose qui n'existe pas encore. En Angleterre, tout ceux qui connaissent cette fiction des années 78 «The Stepford Wives» sauront ce que je veux dire, quoiqu'il était facile de faire la différence entre ces femmes et la réalité dans ce film – mais dans l'avenir, qui sait?

Dans le poème dont je parle, nous n'en sommes pas encore là. Ne soyez pas méfiants envers les autres, simplement parce qu'ils ne sont pas vous. Buvez plutôt une coupe de champagne avec un être humain près de vous et détendez-vous, sachant qu'il est exactement ce qu'il paraît être: s'il marche, parle, mange et dort comme un être humain, c'est un humain – je pense! Bien entendu, l'autre question posée – alors que nous cherchons un véritable être humain – est: est-il bon ou mauvais? Ceci demande plus de recherches... alors, bonne chance!

La Sœur de Descartes

Le célèbre René Descartes était un écrivain Français du dix-septième siècle, Philosophe, Mathématicien reconnu pour de nombreuse nouvelles idées en son temps et aussi pour cette pensée (en latin) «Cogito, ergo sum», autrement dit: «Je pense, donc je suis».

Il était sûrement un homme très intéressant, qui semblait ne pas être certain de sa propre existence. Vous pourriez penser que l'homme invisible avait eu le même problème, quoique cela ne semble pas avoir été sa préoccupation majeure, d'autant plus qu'il n'existait peut-être pas!

Néanmoins, Jeanne, la sœur de René, avait probablement compris que cette pensée de son frère était «la»chose à dire à ce moment-là. Je pense qu'elle savait que René n'avait pas utilisé tout le potentiel de cette pensée et qu'elle devait le faire. Jeanne était sans doute en perpétuelle recherche du mari idéal, noble si possible, et prête à utiliser la fameuse pensée, raisonnablement modifiée, pour son propre usage.

En présence du prétendant possible, elle pouvait par exemple demander: «Suis-je la plus belle femme de France?» et au cas où l réponse n'aurait pas été ce qu'elle espérait, elle aurait pu être capable de poser la question très vite, sans laisser au gentleman le temps de répondre, disant quelque-chose comme «Je pense que je le suis!»

Cela Arrivera

Bon, il semble que nous avons tout fait pour que le futur
soit un désastre, juste parce que nous avons fait ce que
nous aimions pendant trop longtemps. Quand la terre
tout entière est sévèrement affectée par le réchauffement
climatique et ravagée par d' étranges et nouvelles maladies
comme celle causée par le coronavirus de 2020, quelle
chance avons nous d' être capable de vivre ici encore
longtemps?

Tout le monde sait cela je suppose, mais que faisons-nous
pour que ça change? Si nous n'agissons pas rapidement, la
seule solution sera d'aller vivre sur la lune! Un homme y vit
déjà depuis le début mais je doute que beaucoup de gens
aient envie de le rejoindre!

Dans un vieux journal du Dimanche, une rumeur prétendait,
il y a longtemps, qu'Adolf Hitler était parti vivre sur la
lune dans un autobus Londonien. Il semble que cela était
vraiment improbable!

Ce poème est écrit du point de vue de quelqu'un qui est
très fâché que le mauvais temps ait cassé son nain de
jardin, mais est moins concerné par le futur de l'humanité et
des autres animaux bien sûr.

Ce qui est assez désagréable à lire sans doute!

Une Pieuvre Déprimée

C'est étrange, mais il semble que les animaux éprouvent des émotions, tout comme les êtres humains.

Nous avons ici le cas d'une pieuvre très sensible qui s'est sentie insultée par un poisson chat. Le poisson chat a appelé la pieuvre par son nom scientifique, «Octopus vulgaris», mais la pieuvre a interprété le mot «vulgaris» comme une insulte. La pieuvre ne connaissait probablement pas la signification de son nom en Latin, crée par des humains bien sûr.

En tout cas, la solution était claire: la pieuvre devait lutter en ayant l'air plus sophistiquée, ce qu'elle fit en se redressant et en allumant une cigarette Russe.

Quand j'étais jeune, je me souviens d'avoir eu une expérience similaire, en attendant de voir mon premier film X au cinéma local, tenant négligemment une cigarette pendante entre mes lèvres à la façon de John Wayne, pour donner l'impression d'être «cool». Heureusement, il n y avait personne derrière moi pour faire un commentaire!

Si Seulement

Le monde va mal, il en a peut-être toujours été ainsi. Suivant la théorie de Gaia, la terre devrait être capable de soigner elle-même ses maux, selon le stress subit – quoique je doute que cette théorie soit efficace contre le réchauffement climatique.

Mais que dire des gens, ils ne sont jamais d' accord! La théorie de Gaia ne semble pas fonctionner pour eux. Y at-il une autre solution?

Supposons qu'un insecte avec un gros dard ait le pouvoir d'injecter son liquide dans les êtres humains pour les rendre meilleurs, les rendant moins agressifs, moins avares, et en général plus tolérants les uns envers les autres. Supposons que cet insecte puisse se reproduire. La vie serait bien meilleure, sans aucun doute. Est-il vain et naif d'espérer que cela puisse exister? Si seulement!

L' Ordonnance

Tout le monde a entendu parler de ce vieil adage : «une pomme chaque matin éloigne le médecin». En Français nous n' avons pas l' équivalent mais... vous comprenez le sens!

Mais que cela signifie-t-il réellement?

La plus-part d'entre nous pensent que si vous mangez une pomme par jour, vous ne verrez pas souvent le médecin. Quel sens donner à ce proverbe? Peut-être un sens tout différent: si vous donnez des pommes à votre docteur, il sera d'accord pour ne pas vous importuner, après tout, des visites chez le docteur, ou faites par le docteur, ne sont pas une partie de plaisir et comme après chaque visite vous risquez d'avoir attrapé quelque chose, vous préférez rester loin de ses soins médicaux!

Je ne sais pas si tout le monde a essayé cette stratégie pour éviter tout contact non désiré, mais ça vaut la peine d'essayer non? Le poème explique une façon d'y parvenir.

Les Iles Canaries

Vous vous demandez sans doute d'où vient le nom des iles Canaries, quoiqu'il y ait sans doute des choses plus urgentes à faire pour vous en ce moment. Cela semble trop évident. Ce doit être pour la même raison que l'Egypte a été nommée – à cause de tous les œufs (eggs en Anglais) ainsi que la Turkie, à cause de toutes ces dindes ('turkey' en Anglais) courant partout, et le Groenland (Greenland en Anglais) particulièrement vert (green en Anglais).

Pensez-vous qu'il y ait en Chine plus de tasses et de soupières qu'ailleurs?(à cause des porcelaines de Chine).

Quelque chose ne va pas là – dedans semble-t-il, et les iles Canaries ne sont pas l'exception.

Il y a bien des canaris là, mais ce n'est pas l'origine de leur nom. Le poème tente de donner la véritable explication à cette intéressante question.

Une vie sous la Mer

Vous savez ce que c'est quand le monde vous abandonne et échoue à vous donner ce que vous attendez le plus? Oui, moi aussi, et c'est ce qui est arrivé à ma cousine Prue. Elle cherchait un homme qui puisse l'accompagner au cours de sa vie mais hélas, personne d'intéressant ne s'est présenté : sa peau verte n'a sans doute pas favorisé la rencontre.

Un jour, Prue a une étrange idée. Ignorant tous les dangers, elle décide de tenter sa chance en mer et même sous la mer, pensant que la coloration verte de sa peau y prendrait moins d'importance. Elle y rencontre toutes sortes de personnages intéressants, y compris une pieuvre femelle appelée Sue. Le poème décrit la suite de ses aventures dans le lit de la mer.

La Voix dans la Boîte

Il était une fois, au 23eme siècle je pense, alors que la population de Mars était devenue trop faible pour se suffire à elle-même, les Martiens ont eu besoin d'aide pour maintenir l'infrastructure de leurs grandes cités.

Tout naturellement, la planète Terre est apparue comme un bon endroit pour recruter des ouvriers car la contraception avait réduit la quantité de personnel pour travailler sur place. Evidemment, difficile de trouver des volontaires pour aller sur Mars, ils devraient être séduits par la proposition ou bien kidnappés! Le poème explique, si nous sommes capables de comprendre, comment ils ont fait.

Une Heure

Que feriez-vous si vous n'aviez qu'une heure à vivre? Il est évidemment impossible de connaître aussi précisément le temps qu'il nous reste sur cette terre. Mais, ne serait-ce pas merveilleux si cette dernière heure à vivre devenait une fausse prédiction et si vous pouviez survivre avec bonheur de nombreuses années?

Je suggère, que vous ayez raison ou tort, n'importe quand, le jour ou la nuit, il ne peut jamais (du moins je l'espère) être mauvais d'écouter la musique de Serge Rachmaninoff.

J'irai même plus loin, car je crois profondément au pouvoir réparateur de la musique, en disant que si vous sentez la mort frapper à votre porte, vous pourriez être capable de la renvoyer, sa queue entre les jambes, en jouant un des préludes. Un des plus beaux à mon avis, est le prélude en mi bémol majeur opus 23.

Je vous souhaite de vivre longtemps, avec une âme pleine de musique!

Tandis – que Nous Vivons

Je me demande si quelqu'un a déjà essayé d'écrire sur ce sujet......Cela paraît si simple qu'aucune explication ne semble nécessaire, mais en même temps c'est si mystérieusement compliqué qu'aucun langage humain ne peut être capable de le faire. Il semble que les mots n'existent pas. Tout ce que je peux faire c'est de vous offrir ce qui suit.

Tout d'abord, pendant le temps où vous êtes vivant, vous ne vivez évidement qu'une vie –

vous devez donc espérer que ce sera une bonne vie! Si votre vie est une vie heureuse, vous êtes relativement sauvé, en un certain sens, pendant que vous vivez. Vous serez capable de vivre une vie agréable, du début à la fin.

Néanmoins, quand vous mourrez, l'Univers est le même qu'il était avant votre naissance, quand vous n'y étiez pas encore. Mais si vous ni êtes pas, vous courrez le risque d'y arriver encore et vous pouvez espérer arriver dans un endroit sécurisant, bien que ne pouvant pas le contrôler. Bien sûr, ce nouveau «vous» est différent de l'ancien et pourtant ils sont reliés comme le démontre l'explication suivante.

Cela peut vous sembler un total non-sens, mais considérant que pendant que vous vivez il est impossible de renaître, alors que quand vous ne vivez pas encore, vous pouvez naître, quoique dire «encore» ne soit pas tout à fait certain.... bizarre, hein?

Si vous n'arrivez pas à comprendre cela, tournez la page, ou vous pouvez toujours lire une recette de cuisine! Merci!

C'était Là

Ceci est l'étrange histoire d'un événement qui est arrivé le 26 Aout 1998, quelques jours après le décès de la mère de l'auteur, chez elle, à Shoreham by sea, West Sussex.

Si je vous raconte ce qui s'est passé à ce moment-là, vous allez peut-être comprendre.

C'est très tôt le matin, ce Mercredi-là, que cet étrange événement s'est produit, dans la maison où ma mère avait décédé, mais pas dans la même pièce. J'étais prêt à aller me coucher quand j'ai regardé en haut de l'épais rideau qui séparait en deux parties la pièce de devant.

Du milieu approximatif de la tringle à rideaux, un objet argenté et brillant a surgi, comme une pièce de monnaie. Il est resté immobile quelques instants, peut-être une demi-seconde, puis est tombé. Il y avait une grosse différence entre «cette» pièce et n'importe quelle autre pièce existant dans ce monde: elle ne tombait pas verticalement mais en suivant la forme d'un J renversé (comme dans l'illustration). En fait elle semblait tomber sur une petite table de bois près du mur.

J'ai passé quelques minutes à chercher cet objet mais j'ai dû abandonner, très choqué, sans rien avoir trouvé ressemblant à cette pièce. Je me suis trouvé confronté au problème d'aller au lit et de dormir. Si vous avez ce genre d'expérience, c'est beaucoup mieux vers 11 heures du matin, avec des amis qui partagent un bon café et des gâteaux!

Je n'ai jamais pu effacer cette expérience de ma mémoire, cela m'a aidé pour écrire un poème. Juste pour vous...

Courbé sous le Vent

Ceci est un condensé de la vie d'un de mes proches parents. Je l'ai appelé «mon oncle».

C'était un homme spécial, il serait juste de dire que je n'ai jamais rencontré quelqu'un comme lui avant ou après son décès. Je ne me plains pas réellement mais certains pourraient dire qu'il aurait pu faire de grandes choses et être récompensé mais sa vie n'a jamais été ce qu'elle aurait pu être.

Sa vie entière a été une lutte personnelle pour survivre, en un sens, une lutte pour être entendu, une lutte pour réussir, et une vie normale comme la plus part d'entre nous n'était pas suffisante pour lui semble-t-il.

Il était appelé à faire le plus possible, peut-être même dans une autre dimension, quelque chose de perpendiculaire à tout ce que nous connaissons bien. Il était déterminé à laisser une trace qui rappellerait aux générations futures qu'il avait achevé quelque chose de différent.

Ce ne sont pas seulement les vies politiques qui finissent par un échec, mais toutes les vies, au moins dans un certain sens et mon oncle devait aussi quitter la vie pour commencer son chemin «de l'autre côté».

J'espère seulement qu'il trouve cette nouvelle vie agréable.